topps

MATCH ATTAX

ANNUAL 2023

CONTENTS

READY TO PLAY!

Welcome to the official **Match Attax Annual 2023**! It's packed with profiles of the **best players** around, from the G.O.A.T.s to the next generation of footy heroes – turn the pages to meet them! Plus, put your own skills to the test by completing the **tough puzzles and epic activities**. There's loads to keep you busy long after the full-time whistle has blown!

ENGLAND

Here's how the top English clubs fared in Europe over the 2021/22 season!

MANCHESTER CITY

Manchester City's incredible performances and mega-scoring matches saw them top their Champions League group ahead of Paris Saint-Germain. Next, they knocked out Sporting CP and Atlético Madrid, but faced Real Madrid in the semis. An epic 5-6 defeat in extra time was tough to take, but Pep Guardiola's side proved themselves to be one of **Europe's greatest teams**. They bounced back to end the season as back-to-back **league champions**.

STAR PLAYER
KEVIN DE BRUYNE

The **Belgian playmaker** missed a chunk of the season to injury, which affected City's early league form. He came back with a bang on his return, scoring goals and creating assists as if he'd never been away. **Baller.**

STAR PLAYER
MO SALAH

There was just no stopping the **Egyptian King!** A player who's famously racked up five 20-goal seasons since he arrived at Liverpool, Salah didn't disappoint, **netting 31 times** in all competitions. Had it not been for his time away at the African Cup of Nations, he'd likely have scored even more goals!

LIVERPOOL

Free-scoring Liverpool certainly put on a show for their fans, netting goal after goal in the 2021/22 season. In their Champions League group, the Reds breezed to **six wins out of six** – the first time any English club has managed such a feat. They went on to finish as **Champions League runners-up**, losing to Real Madrid in a closely fought final. At home, they pushed Manchester City to the final day of the season taking second place in the league, and earning Champions League football for 2022/23.

CHELSEA

The **2021 Champions of Europe** made an impressive start to the season, losing only once in their Champions League group. With a team that combined seasoned pros like **Thiago Silva** and **Romelu Lukaku**, alongside young stars such as **Trevoh Chalobah** and **Mason Mount**, Chelsea were a side to be feared. The Blues went on to reach the quarter-finals losing in extra time to Real Madrid, while a third-place finish in the league guaranteed more Champions League action for 2022/23. A solid season for Tuchel's team.

STAR PLAYER
JORGINHO

Fresh from winning the Euros with Italy in the summer of 2021, Jorginho brought his top form back to Chelsea. He was the **marshall in the centre of the Blues' midfield**, pulling the strings of a young, talented squad. A Stamford Bridge favourite.

TOTTENHAM HOTSPUR

STAR PLAYER
SON HEUNG-MIN

Spurs' super South Korean played out of his skin, scoring from the first matchday to the last! His **23 goals and seven assists** saw him share the Golden Boot with Salah, while defences felt the full force of his **epic partnership with Kane**.

Tottenham had a truly terrible start to the season. Nuno Espírito Santo was sacked and Spurs sank to the bottom half of the league. Enter super coach Antonio Conte, who turned the team around, as **Harry Kane started scoring again** and Son Heung-Min battled back from injury to become a goal machine! They had a tricky time in Europe and failed to make the knockouts of the Europa Conference League. A fourth-place finish in the league, however, meant that **Spurs qualified for the 2022/23 Champions League** ahead of London neighbours Arsenal. Result!

ARSENAL

Mikel Arteta put his faith in a young squad that included Gabriel Martinelli, Emile Smith Rowe, Bukayo Saka and Eddie Nketiah. A fifth-place league finish saw them just miss out on Champions League footy, but a Europa League spot gave the club a huge boost after a season with no European football.

MANCHESTER UNITED

The return of Cristiano Ronaldo, plus the mega-money signings of Jadon Sancho and Raphaël Varane was meant to bring back the glory years to Old Trafford. But team spirit was crushed and the defence leaked goals. Rangnick replaced Solskjaer but couldn't steady the ship. New coach Erik ten Hag faces a tough task next season.

WEST HAM UNITED

Hammers fans were happy following an incredible season! West Ham finished seventh in the league, but it was in the Europa League where they really shone, making the final four in their first European campaign for over a decade! Declan Rice bossed the midfield, while Jarrod Bowen banged in the goals.

NEXT GEN

JUDE BELLINGHAM

Teen sensation **Jude Bellingham** started out with Birmingham City, making his debut shortly after turning 16. The midfielder registered his first senior goal for the Blues just 63 days after his birthday. His mature performances in the middle of the park quickly caught the attention of some of **Europe's biggest clubs**, and Bellingham departed to join Bundesliga side Borussia Dortmund for £25 million — a world-record transfer fee for a 17-year-old at the time.

Shortly after joining Dortmund, Bellingham became the **youngest English player** to start a Champions League game, in October 2020 v Lazio. He soon cemented his place in the side, thanks to his **dynamic dribbling** and hard work for his team, and remains one of Europe's most-wanted young players.

KEY STATS

POSITION: Midfielder

CLUB: Borussia Dortmund

SQUAD NUMBER: 22

BORN: 29 June, 2003

SEASON:	APPS:	GOALS:
2019/20	44	4
2020/21	46	4
2021/22	44	6

FACT FILE

Bellingham's little bro, Jobe, has followed in Jude's footsteps, also making his Birmingham City debut at the age of just 16.

ARMANDO BROJA

A player who has received glowing praise for his brilliant displays in England, as well as on the international stage, **Armando Broja** is getting better with every game he plays. The young forward from Albania spent the season **on loan to Southampton**, scoring nine goals, but is tipped to return to parent club Chelsea when the 2022/23 season kicks off.

A **natural goalscorer**, Broja can play as a centre forward as well as out wide, where his **strength and speed** cause problems for even the best defenders. A second season in England's top league with some European experience could see Broja become one of Europe's **most dangerous young strikers**, and cause his value to skyrocket. He'd make an excellent addition to Chelsea's attack – you heard it here first!

FACT FILE

Broja became a Blue when he joined Chelsea's Academy from Spurs at the end of his Under-9 season!

KEY STATS

POSITION: Forward

CLUB: Southampton (Chelsea)

SQUAD NUMBER: 18

BORN: 10 September, 2001

SEASON:	APPS:	GOALS:
2019/20	1	0
2020/21	34	11
2021/22	38	9

DANGEROUS DRIBBLE

START

It's time to test just how slick your dribbling skills are. Help PSG hero Messi carry the ball the length of the pitch without being tackled, then get a shot on target!

WATCH OUT FOR DEFENDERS ALONG THE WAY!

FINISH

ANSWERS ON PAGE 70.

SUPER STOPPERS

When it comes to keeping the ball out of the goal, these guys are No.1! Meet four top keepers who had a stellar season.

THIBAUT COURTOIS

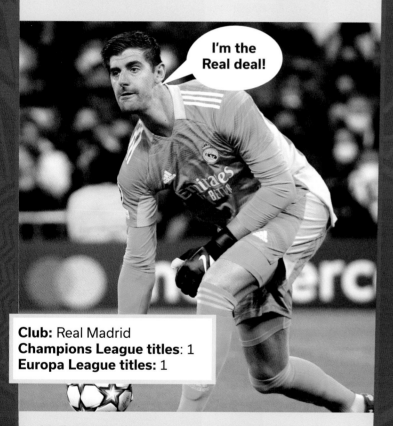

I'm the Real deal!

Club: Real Madrid
Champions League titles: 1
Europa League titles: 1

Mr Real-iable between the posts, Courtois pulls off **key saves match after match**. Madrid's left-footed keeper has won league titles in Belgium, Spain and England, and is blessed with ace technical ability, including amazing reflexes. His performance in the Champions League final in 2022 earned him the player of the match trophy.

MANUEL NEUER

No one gets past Manu!

Club: Bayern Munich
Champions League titles: 2
League titles: 10

One of the **most experienced keepers in world football**, Neuer is still at the top of his game. He's already achieved legendary status at Bayern Munich, playing over 450 games for his Bundesliga club, and twice winning the Champions League. The German great can play with both feet and is an **excellent shot-stopper**. When it comes to penalty shoot-outs, he's happy both saving and scoring!

ALISSON BECKER

Liverpool's brilliant Brazilian keeper Alisson is **top of the league** at keeping clean sheets. His laser-sharp passes always find his teammates, while his quick-thinking has resulted in two assists for Mo Salah. If you're not amazed by that, in 2021, Alisson **scored his first goal** for the Reds, powering in a header from a corner!

Club: Liverpool
Champions League titles: 1
League titles: 5

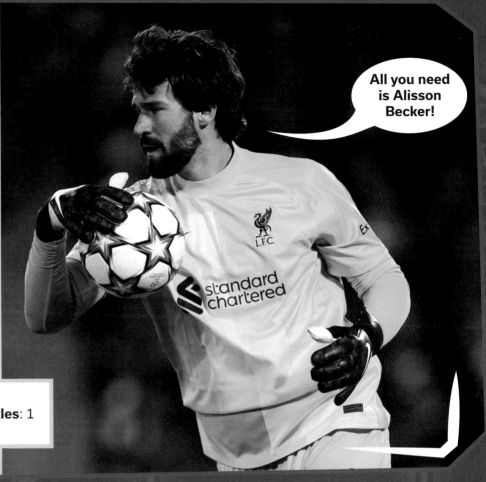

All you need is Alisson Becker!

This superglue is strong stuff!

JAN OBLAK

Atlético Madrid signed Slovenian goalkeeper Jan Oblak in 2014, when he was only 21. Since then, Oblak has proved that he is one of the **best goalkeepers in Europe**, and has helped his club to win both La Liga and Europa League trophies. While Oblak doesn't often play out from the back, he has a knack of always being in the right place at the right time, making spectacular saves look easy. An excellent shot-stopper.

Club: Atlético Madrid
Europa League titles: 1
League titles: 2

MYSTERY MEN

Can you work out who the four Champions League stars are just from their shadows? Use the clues if you get stuck.

1

A I was born in Brazil.

B I've played in one Champions League final.

C My team plays in sky blue.

....

2

A My teammates include Messi and Neymar.

B I turned down Real Madrid in the summer.

C I'm blue through and through!

....

3

A I'm a wizard on the wing.

B My squad number is 20.

C I scored the only goal in the 2022 Champions League final.

....

4

A I switched clubs in the summer.

B My transfer fee was a mega £51.2m.

C Scoring goals is what I do best.

....

ANSWERS ON PAGE 70.

WIN!

A shirt signed by Chelsea midfield ace MASON MOUNT!

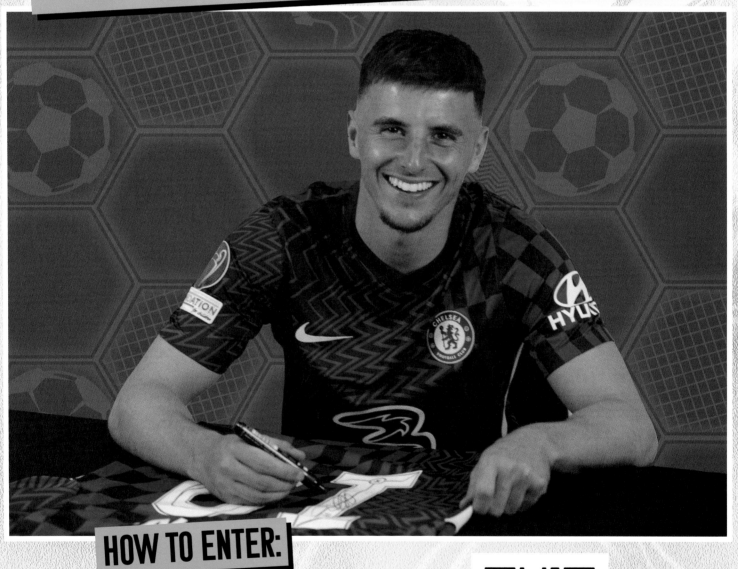

HOW TO ENTER:

Simply scan the QR code or visit uk.topps.com/mountshirtcomp Then tackle the quiz questions for your chance to win!

CHAMPIONS CROSSWORD

These eight greats were all 2021/22 UEFA Champions League quarter-finalists! Read the clues to work out who's who, then fill in the grid with the names of all eight clubs.

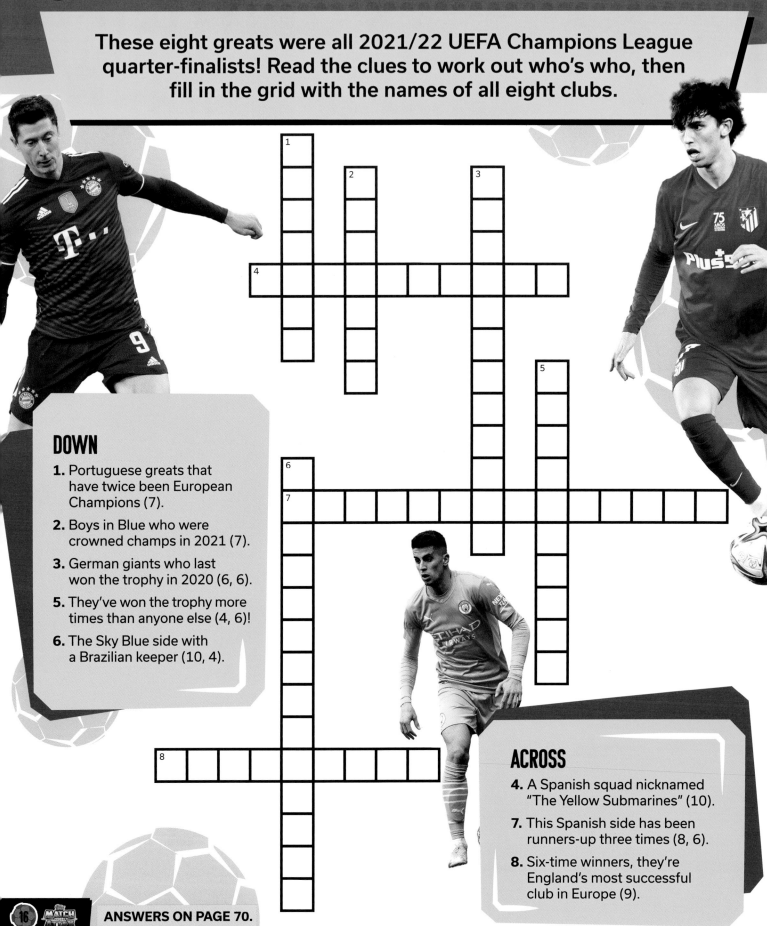

DOWN

1. Portuguese greats that have twice been European Champions (7).

2. Boys in Blue who were crowned champs in 2021 (7).

3. German giants who last won the trophy in 2020 (6, 6).

5. They've won the trophy more times than anyone else (4, 6)!

6. The Sky Blue side with a Brazilian keeper (10, 4).

ACROSS

4. A Spanish squad nicknamed "The Yellow Submarines" (10).

7. This Spanish side has been runners-up three times (8, 6).

8. Six-time winners, they're England's most successful club in Europe (9).

ANSWERS ON PAGE 70.

MASON MOUNT CHELSEA

MID

POWER PLAY

100

14.0M

1

DEFENCE

57

ATTACK

100

100 CLUB

CHAMPIONS LEAGUE

Two of Europe's most decorated club sides met in an epic showdown at the Stade de France, Paris. Real Madrid had won the trophy a record 13 times previously, while Liverpool had six victories. It was the Spanish side's winning mentality that proved decisive, as they dug in to win by a single goal, despite a fearless performance from Liverpool. Vinícius Júnior was the game's only goalscorer, popping up to beat Alisson with a cool second-half strike. The brilliant Brazilian was later named the competition's young player of the season.

The gloves are off!

PLAYER OF THE MATCH

Thibaut Courtois was a man on a mission in goal, keeping out shot after shot from Salah and Mané to claim his first Champions League winner's medal.

2021/22 REVIEW

FINAL
LIVERPOOL   0
REAL MADRID   1

KING KARIM

Real Madrid's No.9 Karim Benzema went on an epic scoring streak in the Champions League, netting two hat-tricks in the knockout rounds, and scoring 15 goals in just 12 games in total! Golden!

MANCHESTER CITY

Manchester City came within minutes of reaching the final, in a memorable semi-final against Real Madrid. At 90 minutes, they had a 5-3 lead, until two goals in two minutes from Real substitute Rodrygo levelled the scores, then an extra-time Benzema penalty saw City shell-shocked. Can Pep Guardiola's side bounce back next season?

VILLARREAL

Winners of the Europa League the previous season, Villarreal surprised many by beating Juventus and Bayern Munich to seal their spot in the last four of the Champions League. There, they fell to an unstoppable Liverpool side, who beat The Yellow Submarine both home and away.

FACT FILE

The last time that Real Madrid lost a Champions League final was way back in 1981!

SPAIN

There were few surprises in Spain in 2021/22 as the big clubs showed up when it mattered!

REAL MADRID

Los Blancos completed another super season, running away with the league title to earn **back-to-back trophies**, and winning a record 14th Champions League title. Massive credit goes to Carlo Ancelotti, who made a surprise return to the Bernabéu in the summer, as well as to Karim Benzema who was on fire all season! New signings David Alaba from Bayern Munich and Eduardo Camavinga from Rennes strengthened the squad.

STAR PLAYER
CASEMIRO

A defensive midfielder with a **fantastic work rate**, Brazilian **Casemiro** completed his eighth season at the club. Ancelotti picked Casemiro whenever fit, rating his **solid passing and reliability**. The tough tackler's 300th appearance in a Madrid shirt came in a Champions League tie in November.

STAR PLAYER
OUSMANE DEMBÉLÉ

Under **new manager Xavi**, the French winger proved just how important he is to the Catalan club as he hit his best form since joining Barça. A **natural sprinter**, Dembélé can shoot with either foot and has the smarts to beat defenders in one-v-ones. He became known in Spain as the "assist king" too!

BARCELONA

2021/22 was possibly the toughest season in Barcelona's history after money troubles saw legend Lionel Messi leave for PSG, while Sergio Agüero was forced to retire after just five games. Their replacements, **Ferran Torres** and **Pierre-Emerick Aubameyang**, hit the ground running, scoring 20 goals between them. A quality midfield that included Gavi and Pedri helped **Barça bounce back** to finish as league runners-up, and after being dumped out of the Champions League, they went on to reach the Europa League's last eight.

ATLÉTICO MADRID

STAR PLAYER
JOÃO FÉLIX

Atleti's record signing at a cool £113m, João Félix found his best form during his third season with the club. The Portuguese forward scored **ten goals and made five assists** before injury ended his season early. This clever young player has a bright future ahead.

Diego Simeone's squad saw a shake-up for the 2021/22 season, with tons of transfers both in and out. Fan fave **Antoine Griezmann** rejoined the club on loan from Barcelona, scoring four goals in the Champions League, while **Rodrigo de Paul** added extra quality to Atleti's midfield. A third-place league finish guaranteed **Champions League football** once again, while in the 2021/22 Champions League they reached the last eight. Manchester City pipped Atleti to the semis following a fiery couple of games.

SEVILLA

The Red-Whites grabbed the final **Champions League spot** with a fourth-place finish in the league. Érik Lamela joined the club and Anthony Martial arrived on loan, but it was young striker **Rafa Mir** who proved to be their **top goal ace**. Sevilla had a tough time in Europe – they failed to get out of their group in the Champions League, while their Europa League competition ended early following a surprise exit in the last 16 to West Ham. Coach Julen Lopetegui will expect more from his squad next season.

STAR PLAYER
JULES KOUNDÉ

A fantastic young defender who's living proof that you don't have to be a giant to play in the centre of defence. Koundé's **speed, aggression and epic heading ability** more than make up for his size, as the Frenchman shows time and again. **A class act.**

21

EDUARDO CAMAVINGA

A player who first starred in the Champions League aged just 16, Real Madrid's midfield ace **Eduardo Camavinga** is a special talent. His skilled first touch and ability to make timely tackles saw Europe's top clubs queuing up to sign him! Camavinga chose a dream move to Real Madrid, with Rennes receiving a **£30 million transfer fee** for the deal.

Despite being the **youngest player in Carlo Ancelotti's squad**, Camavinga showed his class, appearing mostly as a super sub. Nicknamed "Iceman", he coolly competed with Casemiro, Modrić and Kroos for his place, and by the end of his first season in Spain had made 40 appearances and scored twice.

KEY STATS

POSITION: Midfielder

CLUB: Real Madrid

SQUAD NUMBER: 25

BORN: 10 November, 2002

SEASON:	APPS:	GOALS:
2019/20	39	1
2020/21	6	0
2021/22	40	2

FACT FILE

Camavinga made his debut for France aged 17, having moved there when he was two. He could have represented African nations Angola or the Democratic Republic of the Congo.

ALPHONSO DAVIES

When it comes to countries famous for producing the best footballing talent, Canada is possibly not the first nation that springs to mind. Alphonso Davies breaks the mould! The **Ghanaian-born baller** moved to Canada as a refugee, playing for the Vancouver Whitecaps in his adopted country, before joining **German giants Bayern Munich**.

Davies began his career as a left-sided full-back, but can also play further forward as a winger. He can create chances for himself, but more often than not provides assists for teammates, following his roving runs down the left wing and clever crosses. A **Bundesliga and Champions League winner** by the age of 21, Davies has plenty more trophies ahead of him.

FACT FILE

Davies made his debut for Vancouver Whitecaps in the United States' top league at just 15 years old, becoming the second-youngest player to appear in the MLS.

KEY STATS

POSITION: Defender

CLUB: Bayern Munich

SQUAD NUMBER: 19

BORN: 2 November, 2000

SEASON:	APPS:	GOALS:
2019/20	43	3
2020/21	35	1
2021/22	31	0

YOUR
DREAM TEAM
EUROPEAN EDITION

....

1

GK

....

5

CB

....

6

CB

COACH

....

....

....

2

RB

....

3

LB

....

7

CM

....

4

DM

....

8

CM

Which players stood out for you this season? It's time to decide who's earned a place in your dream team. Pick your **ultimate squad** from the teams that competed for **Euro glory** – in the Champions League, Europa League or the Europa Conference League!

9 RW

10 CF

11 LW

SUBS' BENCH

12

13

14

15

16

17

BEST BALLERS
DEFENSIVE WARRIORS

A quality quartet, not much gets past these guys – they love stopping goals as much as strikers love scoring! Which player would you choose to lead your defence?

VIRGIL VAN DIJK

A round of applause for me!

Club: Liverpool
Champions League titles: 1
League titles: 3

Liverpool's captain and probably their most important player, Virgil van Dijk is a **defensive genius**. His cool, calm style of play makes strikers look silly, matching them for pace and **timing tackles to perfection**. Gifted with great technique, he's scored some screamers from set pieces, too. His best moment in a Liverpool shirt was leading them to Champions League glory in 2019.

DAVID ALABA

I reign in Spain!

Club: Real Madrid
Champions League titles: 3
League titles: 11

David Alaba had big boots to fill when he made the move to Real Madrid, and took former captain Ramos's number 4 shirt. The Austrian defender quickly proved to be an excellent signing, bringing **class and experience** to his new side's defence during Real Madrid's **epic Champions League** and Spanish league double.

LEONARDO BONUCCI

Another defender with bags of experience, Bonucci is known for his **tough tackling** and **superb long-range passes**, launching fresh attacks from deep in his own half. His sweet right foot has helped him reach double figures for goals scored, too. The Juventus captain has spent his whole career in Italy, winning nine league titles and has twice been a Champions League runner-up.

Don't call me an Old Lady!

Club: Juventus
Champions League titles: 0
League titles: 9

I'm ace at Marqu-ing!

MARQUINHOS

A hugely **important player** for the French champions, Marquinhos joined Paris Saint-Germain as a teenager, and rose up through the ranks to become their captain in 2020. The Brazilian central defender, who can also play in a defensive midfield role, has now played for the club **over 300 times**. With top technique and plenty of pace, Marquinhos loves to carry the ball out of defence. A defender who rarely puts a foot wrong.

Club: Paris Saint-Germain
Champions League titles: 0
League titles: 7

MATCH ATTAX
TRADING CARD GAME

BAYERN MUNICH

topps

GK

POWER PLAY

100

14.0M

MANUEL NEUER

1

DEFENCE
15

ATTACK
100

100 CLUB

PUZZLE IT OUT!

Can you find the missing footy kit in these picture grids? Draw in the kit so that one of each item appears in every row, column and mini-grid.

1 LEVEL: EUROPA CONFERENCE LEAGUE

2 LEVEL: EUROPA LEAGUE

SYMBOLS:

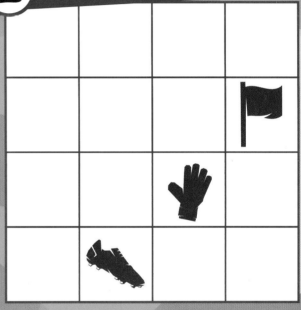

3

LEVEL: CHAMPIONS LEAGUE

SYMBOLS:

ANSWERS ON PAGE 70.

29

The Europa League was full of surprises as two unfancied teams made it all the way to the final in Seville. **Rangers** went ahead with a second-half strike from Jo Aribo, only for **Frankfurt** forward Rafael Borré to level the scores 12 minutes later. **Extra time** was played, but neither team could make the most of their chances. The trophy was decided in a **nail-biting penalty shoot-out**, as Borré was again the hero. Rangers players and fans were left heartbroken at the end of a thrilling string of games in Europe, as **Frankfurt lifted the cup!**

WINNE
UEFA EUROPA LEAGUE

PLAYER OF THE MATCH

Frankfurt keeper **Kevin Trapp** produced a winning save to keep out Aaron Ramsey's penalty in the shoot-out.

EINTRACHT FRANKFURT 1 (5)
RANGERS 1 (4)

WEST HAM UNITED

The Hammers had an epic adventure in Europe, topping their group before beating Sevilla and Lyon to reach the last four – their **first European semi-final for 46 years!** Michail Antonio's goal in the first leg was the side's only goal, as Frankfurt won both matches before going on to win the trophy.

GOLDEN TOUCH

Defender James Tavernier was a shock winner of the competition's golden boot, with seven goals. **What a hero!**

RB LEIPZIG

German side RB Leipzig entered the Europa League after finishing behind Manchester City and Paris Saint-Germain in a tough Champions League group. They came out on top against Atalanta in the quarter-finals, before falling to a **dramatic late Rangers winner** in the semis, in a 3-2 defeat. **Christopher Nkunku** was immense, while **Péter Gulácsi** made some mega saves.

FACT FILE

Rangers' defeat was their fifth in a major European final, with their only victory in 1972.

GERMANY

Bayern were once again too hot to handle in Germany's top flight, ending the season in epic style!

BAYERN MUNICH

Bayern set the pace early on in the Bundesliga and never looked like slowing down. No other team could catch them! Winners of an incredible **tenth title in a row**, Julian Nagelsmann's side finished the season eight points clear of runners-up Dortmund, losing just a handful of matches. Bayern's European form was class too – the club scored maximum points in their Champions League group and went on to reach the semi-finals.

STAR PLAYER
ROBERT LEWANDOWSKI

It was an immense final season at Bayern for **Polish legend Lewandowski** as his performances confirmed his position as the world's best striker. His 35 league goals earned him the **Bundesliga's golden boot** for the seventh time, while he netted 13 times in Europe.

STAR PLAYER
ERLING HAALAND

The **hottest property in world football** right now, Haaland lit up the Bundesliga for three seasons, banging in goal after epic goal for Dortmund. Hungry for a new challenge, the super striker announced a move to Manchester City at the end of the season, the club where his dad once played!

BORUSSIA DORTMUND

Under new manager Marco Rose, Dortmund pushed Munich all the way in the Bundesliga. With a squad packed with talent including **teenager Jude Bellingham**, plus a strong core of German internationals, **Dortmund played some fantastic football**. A third-place finish in their Champions League group saw the German side nicknamed BVB drop into the Europa League, where a memorable win for Rangers ended their hopes of bagging another European trophy.

With a **goal-hungry Moussa Diaby** fed by teenage midfielder **Florian Wirtz**, Bayer's young squad completed another successful season in the Bundesliga. Their third-place finish was their best performance in the league since 2015/16, and guaranteed them a place in the Champions League for 2022/23. This season's European action saw Bayer **top their Europa League group** in December, before going out to Italian side Atalanta in the round of 16.

STAR PLAYER
PATRIK SCHICK

A **strong second season** at Bayer saw Schick score an impressive 24 times, as the forward finished just behind Lewandowski for Bundesliga goals. The Czech has awesome technique and dribbling skills, as well as a **wand of a left foot**.

RB LEIPZIG

A change in manager halfway through the season saw Leipzig's young squad push hard to secure a top four finish in the Bundesliga. New signing **forward André Silva** showed his worth, scoring 18 goals and creating four assists, while captain Péter Gulácsi proved hard to beat in goal. In their Champions League group, Leipzig could not get past heavy hitters Manchester City and PSG, but came close to winning a trophy in the **Europa League** when they reached the semi-finals.

STAR PLAYER
CHRISTOPHER NKUNKU

Attacking midfielder Nkunku put in some **storming performances** on European nights for Leipzig, as well is in the league. He scored seven goals in just six Champions League appearances, and finished the season with an **incredible 35 goals**, not to mention his 16 assists!

NEXT GEN

HARVEY ELLIOTT

A **special talent** with the world at his feet, teenage midfielder Harvey Elliott bounced back from a serious ankle injury to show Liverpool fans just what he can do. Five league appearances and his Champions League debut saw Elliott complete a **strong breakthrough season**, as he slotted in confidently to Jürgen Klopp's star-studded side when selected.

Used mostly on the right as an **attacking midfielder**, Elliott keeps defenders guessing by cutting inside on to his left foot. He's comfortable on the ball, and has **great vision** to pick out teammates with his passing. He proved he can get on the scoresheet himself during a fantastic loan spell with Blackburn Rovers, too. Could the midfield man eventually earn the No.7 shirt in the Reds squad? Watch this space.

KEY STATS

POSITION: Midfielder

CLUB: Liverpool

SQUAD NUMBER: 67

BORN: 4 April, 2003

SEASON:	APPS:	GOALS:
2019/20	8	0
2020/21	43	8
2021/22	11	1

FACT FILE

In 2019, Elliott became the youngest player in Premier League history with his former club, Fulham. He was just 16 years and 30 days old when he made his debut.

GAVI

FACT FILE

Gavi's 95 goals for Real Betis's youth team earned him a move to Barcelona at the age of 11.

A graduate of Barcelona's famous **La Masia academy**, Pablo Martin Páez Gavira, known as "Gavi", was fast-tracked into Barcelona's first team for the 2021/22 season shortly after turning 17. His **sparkling displays in the centre of midfield** proved that the youngster wasn't just there to make up the numbers, though, with Gavi performing beyond his years in the league and in Europe.

Able to play in a number of roles, Gavi has shone brightest as a **central midfielder**, his performances seeing him compared to his Barcelona boss Xavi. If Gavi chooses to stay with the club, his talent could see him become a **first pick for years to come**. If not, a queue of Europe's top clubs will be competing for his signature.

KEY STATS

POSITION: Midfielder

CLUB: Barcelona

SQUAD NUMBER: 30

BORN: 5 August, 2004

SEASON:	APPS:	GOALS:
2021/22	47	2

TOTAL FOOTBALL

These Match Attax cards need an extra stat to make them complete! The attack and defence stats should total 100. Can you work out the missing values and write them in?

1 KYLIAN MBAPPÉ — FOR
DEFENCE: .... — HAT-TRICK HERO — ATTACK: 82 — LIMITED EDITION

2 CRISTIANO RONALDO — FOR
DEFENCE: .... — HAT-TRICK HERO — ATTACK: 80 — LIMITED EDITION

3 ROBERT LEWANDOWSKI — FOR
DEFENCE: .... — HAT-TRICK HERO — ATTACK: 81 — LIMITED EDITION

4 N'GOLO KANTÉ — MID
DEFENCE: .... — ATTACK: 50 — LIMITED EDITION

5

DEF

JOÃO CANCELO

DEFENCE
73

ATTACK
....

LIMITED EDITION

6

Match Attax
TRADING CARD GAME

FOR

JOÃO FÉLIX

DEFENCE
....

HAT-TRICK
HERO

ATTACK
70

LIMITED EDITION

7

LIONEL MESSI

FOR

DEFENCE
....

HAT-TRICK
HERO

ATTACK
83

LIMITED EDITION

FACT FILE

Messi has scored an epic 55 hat-tricks during his career, while Ronaldo has reached 60. Incredible!

8

DEF

DAYOT UPAMECANO

DEFENCE
71

ATTACK
....

LIMITED EDITION

9

DEF

JULES KOUNDÉ

DEFENCE
68

ATTACK
....

LIMITED EDITION

ANSWERS ON PAGE 70.

MIDFIELD MASTERS

From perfect passers to awesome assist-makers, here's who pulls the strings for their sides from the middle of the park.

JORGINHO

Time for my masterclass!

Club: Chelsea
Champions League titles: 1
Europa League titles: 1

A **classy midfielder** and leader in the Chelsea side, Jorginho's brilliant footballing brain helps him stay one step ahead of the opposition. The Brazilian-born Italian's game is all about **keeping possession** for his side and controlling the tempo, before unleashing the the perfect pass. A fabulous number 5.

LUKA MODRIĆ

Luka me go!

Club: Real Madrid
Champions League titles: 5
League titles: 6

When it comes to world-class ballers, this guy is the **Real deal**! While the mega midfield man may be in the final seasons of an incredible career, he's still bossing the Bernabéu and tearing up the Champions League with his **pinpoint passes** and **jaw-dropping touches**. Promise you'll never retire, Luka!

FRENKIE DE JONG

It took a little time for Frenkie de Jong to find his feet when he first signed for Barcelona, but the young midfielder has been in **flying form** under new manager Xavi. A player who can perform many midfield roles, de Jong has the talent to follow in his manager's footsteps and become a legend in Spain. **A quality baller.**

Club: Barcelona
Champions League titles: 0
League titles: 1

I was born to play for Barça!

Thanks Verr-y much!

MARCO VERRATTI

A **dynamic dribbler** and **tireless runner**, Marco Verratti has now spent ten seasons in the French capital with Paris Saint-Germain. While his side's famous forwards grab the headlines, the Italian playmaker is the **spark in the centre of PSG's midfield**, crafting perfect passes for his teammates.

Club: Paris Saint-Germain
Champions League titles: 0
League titles: 8

WOMEN'S CHAMPIONS LEAGUE

With mega match-ups and record crowds, the women's edition of the Champions League 2021/22 was epic until the final whistle! A fabulous final saw Lyon win back the trophy in style.

LYON

Winners of the Champions League a **record eight times**, Lyon were determined to reclaim their crown as the queens of Europe. Having swept aside Juventus and Paris Saint-Germain on their way to the final, **Lyon were fearless** against Barcelona. Three first-half goals from Amandine Henry (a screamer), Ada Hegerberg (who else?) and Catarina Macario (a tap-in) stunned Barcelona. Sonia Bompastor became the first woman to win the competition as both player and coach. Legends!

STAR PLAYER
ADA HEGERBERG

Six times a Champions League winner, Hegerberg is also the competition's **all-time top scorer**. The Norwegian forward has scored an incredible 59 goals and counting, six of those in finals, including a **hat-trick** in the 2019 decider. Having sat out most of 2020 and 2021 through injury, Hegerberg was happy to hit her best form again.

STAR PLAYER
ALEXIA PUTELLAS

FIFA Women's Player of the Year 2022 Putellas has been in unbelievable form over the past few seasons. An amazing captain, she has an eye for goal and an **unstoppable left foot**! Her 11 goals in the 2021/22 Champions League won her the **Golden Boot**, but she'd have preferred a winner's medal.

BARCELONA

Favourites to win back-to-back trophies for the first time in their history, Barcelona began their Champions League tournament with a bang, topping their group, before **thrashing Real Madrid and Wolfsburg** in the knockouts. With players who can score from all over the pitch, they looked like the team to beat, but Barça got a shock when they came up against Lyon in the final. The Spanish side never recovered after Lyon raced into a 3-0 lead, with Alexia Putellas' strike a token goal.

WOLFSBURG

After beating English sides Chelsea and Arsenal on their way to the Champions League semi-finals, Wolfsburg eventually came unstuck against defending champions Barcelona. A 5-1 defeat in front of a record crowd at Camp Nou in the first leg saw Wolfsburg unable to recover, despite winning the return fixture. **Tabea Wassmuth provided Wolfsburg's firepower**, scoring ten Champions League goals in total, while **Almuth Schult** pulled off some fine saves.

STAR PLAYER
JILL ROORD

A midfielder who made the move from Arsenal in summer 2021, Roord had an excellent first season in Germany. She scored **important Champions League goals** to help Wolfsburg reach the semis and provided defensive cover too.

PARIS SAINT-GERMAIN

STAR PLAYER
MARIE-ANTOINETTE KATOTO

A **dangerous dribbler** with **pace to burn**, PSG's striker known as "MAK" is a menace to any defence. By the age of 21, she'd already scored **100 goals** for the Red and Blues thanks to her fantastic finishing skills. Katoto's seven goals in the Champions League in 2021/22 guided PSG to the final four of the competition.

Having lost Champions League finals in 2015 and 2017, PSG were aiming to go one better in Europe's elite club competition. The Paris side started well, sailing through the group stage without letting in a single goal! In the last eight, **Ramona Bachmann's cool strike in extra time** pipped Bayern Munich to a semi-final place where they faced French rivals Lyon. Katoto scored first for PSG, and again in the second leg, but her goals were not enough to beat seven-time champions Lyon.

MORE EURO HEROES

From outstanding stoppers to great goal-getters, we put eleven more superstars of the Women's Champions League under the spotlight.

GOALKEEPER

CHRISTIANE ENDLER
LYON

The top Chilean keeper switched from PSG to Lyon in search of her first Champions League medal and made important saves to help her new side stop Barcelona's attack in the final. She also picked up two French league titles in a row.

ASHLEY LAWRENCE
PARIS SAINT-GERMAIN

Canadian Lawrence put in some fantastic performances at full-back as PSG came out on top against Real Madrid and Bayern Munich. Her speed and willingness to attack set her apart from the competition.

WENDIE RENARD
LYON

A towering defender and legendary captain, Renard has won an incredible eight Champions League winner's medals. She scored in both legs of the semi-final against PSG to book Lyon's place in the final in 2022.

IRENE PAREDES
BARCELONA

Paredes moved back to Spain in 2021 and formed a solid partnership with Mapi Leon in Barca's back line. The transfer paid off as Paredes won her third league title and played in a Champions League final!

DEFENDERS

MIDFIELDERS

PERNILLE HARDER
CHELSEA

Harder has been huge in the Champions League season after season, but is yet to get her hands on the trophy. Her dreams were put on hold for another season following Chelsea's early exit.

SELMA BACHA
LYON

Lyon's young left-winger finished top of the Champions League assists table at the tender age of 21! Brilliant Bacha helped Lyon reach the final, where she won her fourth winner's medal.

SAKI KUMAGAI
BAYERN MUNICH

Equally solid in defence and midfield, Kumagai was ever-present for Bayern, as the German side made the last eight. She even popped up with the winner against former club Lyon.

AITANA BONMATÍ
BARCELONA

This exciting young attacker blasted on to the European stage in 2021, scoring in the Champions League final. Her player-of-the-match performances led Barcelona to back-to-back finals.

VIVIANNE MIEDEMA
ARSENAL

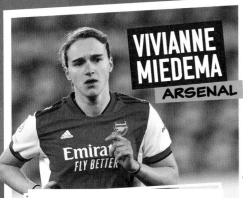

Despite playing in a deeper role under coach Jonas Eidevall, Miedema netted seven superb Champions League goals to help the Gunners reach the quarter-finals. Scoring goals is in her DNA!

CAROLINE GRAHAM HANSEN
BARCELONA

The form of forward Graham Hansen has been key to Barcelona's rapid rise to the top. A creator and scorer of goals, the Norwegian has top technique and loves to take on defenders.

SAM KERR
CHELSEA

Although Chelsea suffered a shock exit in the group stage on goal difference, super striker Sam Kerr was a bright spark in the Blues' side, scoring four times in six matches.

FORWARDS

Match Attax
TRADING CARD GAME

Topps

BAYERN MUNICH

JOSHUA KIMMICH

MID

POWER PLAY
100

14.0M

1

DEFENCE
100

ATTACK
79

100 CLUB

ASSIST KINGS

When it comes to creating chances for teammates, these big-game players always deliver. Find their last names in the grid – they can read forwards, backwards, up, down and diagonally. Then connect each player to the right club.

D	B	A	P	J	K	E	F	B	N	Y	C	F	R
F	E	R	N	A	N	D	E	S	J	G	S	O	T
H	L	E	W	T	O	S	L	Q	A	O	I	P	X
Y	L	G	F	I	D	M	I	D	I	N	J	D	G
J	I	F	Q	C	N	E	X	P	U	Q	E	B	U
R	N	D	X	I	P	R	B	J	T	C	V	M	V
U	G	Z	S	P	H	D	S	R	Z	W	R	I	F
P	H	R	A	Z	T	U	J	C	U	L	K	S	D
K	A	B	N	I	I	H	X	T	D	Y	H	S	Y
U	M	Y	L	C	Q	Y	S	M	H	D	N	I	N
T	Z	Q	I	M	W	Z	C	V	I	A	T	E	O
A	S	N	X	P	B	F	R	M	E	P	J	G	T
F	I	D	V	Z	S	A	L	A	H	Q	S	L	N
V	H	E	L	E	B	M	E	D	G	D	N	S	A

ANTONY	REAL MADRID
Jude BELLINGHAM	BARCELONA
Kevin DE BRUYNE	PARIS SAINT-GERMAIN
Ousmane DEMBÉLÉ	LIVERPOOL
Bruno FERNANDES	BAYERN MUNICH
João FÉLIX	AJAX
VINÍCIUS JÚNIOR	MANCHESTER CITY
Kylian MBAPPÉ	MANCHESTER UNITED
Mohamed SALAH	ATLÉTICO MADRID
Leroy SANÉ	BORUSSIA DORTMUND

ANSWERS ON PAGES 70-71.

45

ITALY

It was all change in Italy as Milan were No.1, while no club could reach the quarter-finals of the top European competitions.

AC MILAN

In a nail-biting end to the season, AC Milan were crowned champions for the first time in **over a decade**! They may not have scored the most goals, but they won more times than anyone else, pipping city neighbours Inter to the league title. With plenty of experience up front, **Simon Kjaer** and **Theo Hernandez shone in defence**, while **Franck Kessie** remained on the radar of many top clubs.

STAR PLAYER
FIKAYO TOMORI

Following a successful loan spell the previous season, **Tomori joined AC Milan for £25m** in June 2021. With pace, pressing, plus excellent positioning, the centre-back has kicked on to become a **regular starter** for Milan. Chelsea may regret letting the centre-back go too soon!

STAR PLAYER
LAUTARU MARTÍNEZ

INTER MILAN

Argentine centre-forward Martínez was the **club's top scorer** for the season, netting 25 times. Among them were some important goals, including Inter's winner in a Champions League last-16 tie against Liverpool. Martínez's game is all about goals, whether he's playing as a No.10 or as an out-and-out striker.

On the blue side of the city, Inter Milan had to settle for second place and see their rivals lift the league trophy. With Lukaku sold to Chelsea, it was up to Lautaro Martínez and Edin Džeko to provide the firepower, as Inter finished the season as **Italy's highest-scoring club**. Champions League nights had Inter fans dreaming of silverware, but their hopes were ended by Liverpool in the last 16.

NAPOLI

Returning manager **Luciano Spalletti** masterminded a strong start to the season as the Blues **won nine of their first ten** league matches. A third-place finish guaranteed their Champions League qualification. Record signing Victor Osimhen led the goal-scoring charts, with 18 goals, with Mertens and Di Lorenzo chipping in too. In the Europa League, they finished second in their group, but faced an in-form Barcelona in the knockouts, who were just too strong.

STAR PLAYER
KALIDOU KOULIBALY

Considered by many to be one of the **best all-round defenders** in world football, Koulibaly is a tall but graceful centre-back who loves to play the ball.

JUVENTUS

STAR PLAYER
MATTHIJS DE LIGT

Once the Golden Boy of Ajax, centre-back de Ligt has **grown up to become a top defender**. His third season at Juve was his best yet – the young defender put in some awesome performances in the Champions League, stopping some of Europe's best forwards in their tracks.

Desperate to reclaim their league crown, Juventus had a disappointing start to the season, eventually recovering to finish fourth. With legends Buffon and Ronaldo having left the club, it was up to **new stars** such as **Manuel Locatelli** and **Moise Kean** to impress. After topping their group in the Champions League, Juventus's European campaign ended in the round of 16, where Villarreal ran out as convincing winners.

NEXT GEN

RYAN GRAVENBERCH

When Frenkie de Jong left Ajax, the club was lucky enough to have the perfect **ready-made replacement** in young central midfielder Ryan Gravenberch. Ryan made his league debut aged 16 years and 130 days – **the youngest ever player to feature in the Dutch Eredivisie**, and played in the Champions League that same season.

Tall but agile, Gravenberch loves to **drive from deep**, and keep hold of the ball in the tightest of spaces. He gets on the scoresheet a few times a season, too – it was no wonder he was a wanted man by a host of Champions League clubs. Expect to see the Dutchman dazzle at new club Bayern Munich in 2022/23.

KEY STATS

POSITION: Midfielder

CLUB: Bayern Munich

SQUAD NUMBER: 8

BORN: 16 May, 2002

SEASON:	APPS:	GOALS:
2019/20	12	3
2020/21	47	5
2021/22	42	3

FACT FILE

Gravenberch reached 100 appearances for Ajax while still a teenager!

COLE PALMER

Able to **operate in midfield** or as a **striker**, Cole Palmer has risen through the ranks at Manchester City to claim a place in their **world-class Champions League squad**. His **first goal** in the competition came against Bruges in the group stage after just two minutes on the pitch!

A foot injury kept him out of the side for months at the start of 2022, but Palmer found his way back to full fitness for the season end to help secure his **first league title**. Under super coach Pep Guardiola, Palmer believes his boyhood club is the perfect place to build his career and win even more trophies.

FACT FILE

When he made City's first-team squad, Palmer felt starstruck playing alongside his heroes.

KEY STATS

POSITION: Midfielder

CLUB: Manchester City

SQUAD NUMBER: 80

BORN: 6 May, 2002

SEASON:	APPS:	GOALS:
2020/21	2	0
2021/22	11	3

WORLDIES!

CHAMPIONS LEAGUE GOALS OF THE SEASON

There were plenty of first-class finishes in this season's UEFA Champions League, from victorious volleys to heroic headers! Colour in the footballs to rate these eight epic goals.

For goal clips and highlights visit **UEFA.COM/ UEFACHAMPIONSLEAGUE**

BAYERN MUNICH v DYNAMO KYIV

Robert Lewandowski's cool-as-ice bicycle kick in the Kyiv snow.

YOUNG BOYS v ATALANTA

Duván Zapata's deadly turn and volley to open the scoring in a 3-3 group stage draw.

MANCHESTER CITY v RB LEIPZIG

Jack Grealish's curled corker on his Champions League debut.

BARCELONA v DYNAMO KYIV

Ansu Fati's quality finish that clinched three points in the group stage.

RB LEIPZIG v PARIS SAINT-GERMAIN

Christopher Nkunku's diving header to earn a draw with his old club, PSG.

REAL MADRID v INTER MILAN

Marco Asensio's effort hit both posts before finding the roof of the net. Pinball perfection!

PARIS SAINT-GERMAIN v MANCHESTER CITY

Leo Messi's edge-of-the box strike that sent the crowd wild in Paris.

MANCHESTER CITY v SPORTING CP

Raheem Sterling's stunning shot in a memorable match at the Etihad. Top bins!

WE'VE MISSED YOU!

**Topps events are back this October
and we can't wait to meet you!**
Our events give you the chance to meet other collectors, learn and play
Match Attax against each other, plus the opportunity to win prizes
and see some special guests!

Find out if we'll be at a venue near YOU by checking our website.
See uk.topps.com/events

#THECHASEISON

Match Attax has more epic chase cards to find than ever before, including genuine autographs!
Post your best pulls on social media with the **#THECHASEISON** to win some incredible prizes including UEFA Champions League match tickets!

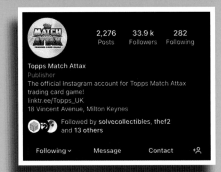

Instagram

TikTok

Twitter

Facebook

GET CREATING ON OUR SOCIAL CHANNELS!

FINAL DESTINATION

Can you remember which stadium hosted the epic Champions League final in 2022? Follow the lines to find out.

Allianz Arena

Wembley Stadium

Stade de France

ANSWER ON PAGE 71.

Topps

PARIS SAINT-GERMAIN

NEYMAR JR

FOR

POWER PLAY

100

14.0M

DEFENCE

46

ATTACK

100

100 CLUB

It all went to plan for PSG in France's top division as they stormed to the title.

FRANCE

PARIS SAINT-GERMAIN

With a host of dream signings joining the club – **Messi, Donnarumma and Sergio Ramos** among them – Paris Saint-Germain led the French league for almost the entire season, winning with four games to go. In the Champions League, **Mbappé and Messi boasted 11 goals between them**, as PSG reached the last 16. There, Mauricio Pochettino's side were knocked out by an unstoppable Real Madrid and a brilliant Benzema hat-trick.

STAR PLAYER
KYLIAN MBAPPÉ

In a squad full of megastars, it's hard to pick just one, but **Kylian Mbappé** outshone Messi and Neymar all season as PSG's stand-out star. He was their leading scorer (36 goals), and made the most appearances too, while his explosive pace left defenders for dead in France as well as the Champions League!

STAR PLAYER
AURÉLIEN TCHOUAMÉNI

Young France star Tchouaméni was **dynamite in Monaco's midfield,** always eager to win back the ball for his side. His timely tackles and interceptions saw him rank alongside Europe's best players. Clubs from England were reportedly chasing his signature, but Tchouaméni chose a move to European champs Real Madrid.

MONACO

Monaco's end to the season was nothing less than sensational as they bagged the runners-up spot in the French league on goal difference! **Super striker** and **captain Ben Yedder scored 31 times** for his side, while Henrique and Volland made the most assists. In Europe, Monaco dropped out of the Champions League in qualifying, but went on to reach the last 16 of the Europa League, where they were beaten by Braga. What a season!

MARSEILLE

While PSG ran away with the league, Marseille led the chasing pack for most of the season, only to slip to third place in the final fortnight. **Polish loan star Arkadiusz Milik** was the club's leading scorer with 20 goals, while **Dimitri Payet** showed his experience and quality. A poor placing in their Europa League group saw Marseille drop down to the Europa Conference League where they reached the semi-finals.

STAR PLAYER
WILLIAM SALIBA

Saliba spent the season on loan to Marseille from parent club Arsenal to gain some **much-needed minutes** on the pitch. The French defender who only **turned 21 in 2022** was a sensation, making 52 appearances in his home country. Expect to see Saliba's first league appearances in an Arsenal shirt in 2022/23.

RENNES

STAR PLAYER
MARTIN TERRIER

Rennes No.7 Terrier enjoyed his best ever season in front of goal, scoring 21 times. Playing as a **second striker**, he netted some important goals for the Red and Blacks, including his first Rennes hat-trick. Whether it's a chance in the box or a shot from range, talented attacker Terrier doesn't mind how he scores, as long as he helps the team.

The **final Champions League qualification spot** was earned by Rennes, who grabbed fourth place in the league, in an exciting end to the season. Despite being hit with injuries, captain Hamari Traoré rallied his troops and the Rennes squad battled on. Their adventure in the **Europa Conference League** saw them reach the last 16, where Leicester City sneaked through 3-2 over two hard-fought games.

PEDRI

Pedro González López, known as **"Pedri"**, is another of Barcelona's teenage heroes. The talented playmaker can play with both feet, make dazzling runs and deliver a killer final ball. He made his **La Liga debut aged 16** for Canary Island club Las Palmas, before being snapped up by Barcelona at the end of his first pro season.

By 18, Pedri was playing out of his skin, his magical displays putting him among the **top 20 players** in the world. While injury limited his appearances in 2021/22, Pedri still managed to beat his goals total for a season, scoring five times for Barça. In October he was rewarded with a new contract with a rumoured release clause of a **record €1 billion**! A player with a future brighter than the Spanish sun!

FACT FILE

When he's not in action, Pedri loves playing basketball or FIFA on his Xbox – he always chooses to play as Barça!

KEY STATS

POSITION: Midfielder

CLUB: Barcelona

SQUAD NUMBER: 16

BORN: 25 November, 2002

SEASON:	APPS:	GOALS:
2019/20	37	4
2020/21	52	4
2021/22	22	5

FLORIAN WIRTZ

Google "whizzkid" and a picture of Bayer Leverkusen's Florian Wirtz may well pop up! A **dynamic midfielder** who can operate on the wing or deeper in midfield, Wirtz showed no sign of nerves when he made his league debut as a 17-year-old. Since then, he's made himself a **key member of the first team** at Leverkusen, putting in some epic performances in the league and in Europe.

In the 2021/22 season, Wirtz's second full campaign, the teenager hit **double figures for goals as well as assists**, and became the **youngest player to reach 50 Bundesliga appearances** back in December. Leverkusen will be desperate to hold on to their brightest player in a generation as interest from a host of clubs in Europe's top leagues grows.

FACT FILE

Wirtz's older sister Juliane also plays pro football for Leverkusen, in the Women's Bundesliga.

KEY STATS

POSITION: Midfielder

CLUB: Bayer Leverkusen

SQUAD NUMBER: 27

BORN: 3 May, 2003

SEASON:	APPS:	GOALS:
2019/20	9	1
2020/21	38	8
2021/22	31	10

TASTY TIE

The UEFA Champions League quarter-finals saw some of Europe's top sides paired together. Kylian Mbappé's goals in each leg for PSG were not enough to get past the mighty Madrid!

How quickly can you spot five things that are different in the second picture? Cross out a ball for each difference you find.

ANSWERS ON PAGE 71.

GOAL MACHINES

Check out these epic goalscorers – four forwards who simply can't stop scoring! Who would you select to start up front?

NEYMAR JR

Come closer if you wanna be 'megged!

Club: Paris Saint-Germain
Champions League titles: 1
League titles: 8

A player with **mind-blowing skills**, Neymar is part of **PSG's dream forward line** alongside Mbappé and Messi. His fifth season in the French capital may have been his leanest yet for goals scored (12), but the Brazilian is capable of producing the magical moment in any match to earn three points for his side. Neymar's next goal is trying to win the **Champions League** for his French fans.

DUŠAN VLAHOVIĆ

I score when I want!

Club: Juventus
Champions League titles: 0
League titles: 1

One of the signings of the season, Dušan Vlahović joined Juventus from Fiorentina in the January transfer window and made an **instant impact**, scoring 20 goals in his first 24 games. The Serbian striker is **deadly from close range**, as he outmuscles defenders on the ground and in aerial duels. Vlahović couldn't wait to score his first Champions League goal, netting after just **32 seconds** on his debut!

KARIM BENZEMA

Loving his role as the **main man at Real Madrid**, Karim Benzema is the third-highest all-time scorer behind club legends Cristiano Ronaldo and Raul with over 300 goals. A forward with awesome technique and flawless finishing, the Frenchman gets better with age. 2021/22 was his best goal-scoring season ever, with an epic 44 in 46 games, including **two Champions League hat-tricks**!

Can't wait to watch that one back on YouTube!

Club: Real Madrid
Champions League titles: 5
League titles: 8

HARRY KANE

On me 'ead, Sonny!

The England striker was not at his sparkling best during the first half of the season, after Manchester City had an enormous bid to take him to the Etihad rejected. Things quickly changed though under new manager Antonio Conte, and **Kane found his shooting boots** again. Spurs' captain finished the season with 26 goals, while his strike partnership with Son Heung-Min set a new record – the pair had combined to score an incredible 41 times in the league by 1st May.

Club: Tottenham Hotspur
Champions League titles: 0
League titles: 0

EURO ROUND-UP

SCOTLAND

Rangers and Celtic played cat and mouse in a thrilling title chase!

CELTIC

It was a **season of two halves** for Celtic as an almost entirely new group of players took time to find their feet. Then in January Celtic took the No.1 spot in the Scottish Premiership and didn't give it up again! Goalkeeper **Joe Hart was outstanding**, keeping 19 clean sheets in the league, while Japan ace **Kyogo Furuhashi** led the Hoops' list of top scorers. Celtic entered the Europa Conference League in the knockout round play-offs, but were well beaten by Danish side Bodo/Glimt.

STAR PLAYER
CALLUM MCGREGOR

A natural leader, McGregor was given the **captain's armband** in the summer and had an incredible season. Skippering Celtic to their 52nd league title was one of the midfielder's proudest moments. His ability to **launch his team's attacks** is one of McGregor's greatest strengths, while his defensive play is just as important too. A player at the heart of Celtic's success.

STAR PLAYER
JAMES TAVERNIER

Englishman Tavernier proved once again just how important he is to Rangers, making 58 appearances and scoring 18 goals – **an incredible return for a defender**! His assists record is equally epic. The roving right-back has now completed seven seasons at Rangers, captaining the side for the last four.

RANGERS

Matching their heroics of the previous season, where Rangers went unbeaten in the league, was always going to be a tall order, but the Blues made a **stunning start** to the new campaign. Even when manager Steven Gerrard left for Aston Villa in November, Rangers stood firm at the top of the table. Points were dropped in January and a 3-0 loss to Celtic in February put their Glasgow rivals in pole position. An epic effort to make the **final of the Europa League** gave fans something to cheer about.

HEARTS

Hearts were on terrific form for the whole season, never dropping out of the **top three teams**. Finishing third earned them the chance to qualify for the Europa League Conference for the season ahead. Northern Irish striker **Liam Boyce led the line**, scoring 16 goals, while top keeper Craig Gordon returned to his boyhood club. A solid season.

JOHN SOUTARR

Centre-back Soutarr was a **big performer** for Hearts after battling back from a number of serious injuries over the past few years. Possessing good pace for a defender, Soutarr loves to carry the ball up the pitch, while Hearts fans admire his **defensive grit**. His impressive form saw Soutarr move to rivals Rangers at the end of the season, after seven years at Tynecastle.

DUNDEE UNITED

Dundee United clinched fourth place in the league to book their entry to the Europa Conference League third round for 2022/23. It was a brilliant reward for the squad's hard work, and their highest league finish in nine years! **Nicky Clark was the club's top scorer** with ten goals – the only player in the squad to reach double figures, while young midfielder **Dylan Levitt quickly became a fan favourite**, on loan from Manchester United.

IAN HARKES

American attacking midfielder Harkes scored some **crucial goals** in the league that saw Dundee United make a charge for a European place. His epic header against champions Celtic and the winner in the Dundee derby sent the Tangerines fans wild! It's no wonder Harkes was voted the club's player of the year. 2022/23 will give Harkes his first taste of European football.

CELEBRATIONS RATED!

When the ball hits the back of the net, these players aren't shy to celebrate! Check out some of the best goal salutes in the game, then rate all six to see whose celebration comes out on top.

FIST BUMP

Goal ace Robert Lewandowski "knuckled down" to come up with his latest trademark goal celebration. **Double fist-bumping himself** proved perfect when hugging teammates wasn't encouraged due to Covid-19. Clever!

MY RATING:

☆☆☆☆☆

SLIDE SHOW

Kylian Mbappé's classic **knee slide** with his arms folded is a surefire way of getting PSG fans off their seats. Simple but effective, how would you rate this one?

MY RATING:

☆☆☆☆☆

FLIPPING AMAZING!

Chelsea striker Sam Kerr saves her acrobatic goal celebration for big games or special strikes. Can any celebration beat a **backflip**?

MY RATING:
☆☆☆☆☆

LOOKING UP

When Messi finds the back of net, he frequently **points to the sky**. The customary celebration is in honour of his grandma, who passed away before Messi became a footballing legend.

MY RATING:
☆☆☆☆☆

EYE FOR GOAL

Manchester City striker Ellen White pulls out her epic **"goggles"** goal celebration in honour of her hero, French striker Anthony Modeste.

MY RATING:
☆☆☆☆☆

SAY YES!

Ronaldo's celebration is one of the most recognised in football. The forward performs a mid-air pirouette before landing with his arms straight by his sides, while shouting **"siuuu"** (Spanish for "yes"). Loved by Madrid and Man United fans alike!

MY RATING:
☆☆☆☆☆

ANSWERS

PAGES 10-11 DANGEROUS DRIBBLE

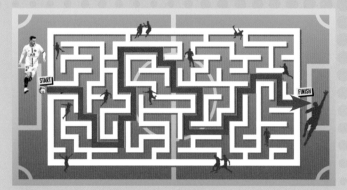

PAGE 14 MYSTERY MEN

1. Ederson
2. Kylian Mbappé
3. Vinícius Júnior
4. Erling Haaland

PAGE 16 CHAMPIONS CROSSWORD

DOWN

1. BENFICA
2. CHELSEA
3. BAYERN MUNICH
5. REAL MADRID
6. MANCHESTER CITY

ACROSS

4. VILLARREAL
7. ATLÉTICO MADRID
8. LIVERPOOL

PAGE 29 PUZZLE IT OUT!

1.
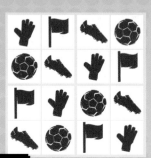

2.
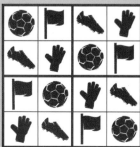

3.

PAGES 36-37 TOTAL FOOTBALL

1. 18 defence
2. 20 defence
3. 19 defence
4. 50 defence
5. 27 attack
6. 30 defence
7. 17 defence
8. 29 attack
9. 32 attack

PAGE 45 ASSIST KINGS

D	B	A	P	J	K	E	F	B	N	Y	C	F	R
F	E	R	N	A	N	D	E	S	J	G	S	O	T
H	L	E	W	T	O	S	L	Q	A	O	I	P	X
Y	L	G	F	I	D	M	I	D	I	N	J	D	G
J	I	F	Q	C	N	E	X	P	U	Q	E	B	U
R	N	D	X	I	P	R	B	J	T	C	V	M	V
U	G	Z	S	P	H	D	S	R	Z	W	R	I	F
P	H	R	A	Z	T	U	J	C	U	L	K	S	D
K	A	B	N	I	I	H	X	T	D	Y	H	S	Y
U	M	Y	L	C	Q	Y	S	M	H	D	N	I	N
T	Z	O	I	M	W	Z	C	V	I	A	T	E	O
A	S	N	X	P	B	F	R	M	E	P	J	G	T
F	I	D	V	Z	S	A	L	A	H	Q	S	L	N
V	H	E	L	E	B	M	E	D	G	D	N	S	A